EMMANUEL JOSEPH

The Heart's Algorithm, A Story of Career Choices, Romantic Bonds, and Spiritual Growth

Copyright © 2025 by Emmanuel Joseph

All rights reserved. No part of this publication may be reproduced, stored or transmitted in any form or by any means, electronic, mechanical, photocopying, recording, scanning, or otherwise without written permission from the publisher. It is illegal to copy this book, post it to a website, or distribute it by any other means without permission.

First edition

This book was professionally typeset on Reedsy. Find out more at reedsy.com

Contents

1	Chapter 1: Beginnings in the City	1
2	Chapter 2: The Tech Startup	3
3	Chapter 3: Navigating Love and Ambitions	4
4	Chapter 4: Spiritual Awakening	6
5	Chapter 5: Challenges and Resilience	7
6	Chapter 6: Finding Balance	8
7	Chapter 7: New Beginnings	9
8	Chapter 8: The Power of Connection	10
9	Chapter 9: Overcoming Adversity	11
10	Chapter 10: Celebrating Success	12
11	Chapter 11: Giving Back	13
12	Chapter 12: A New Horizon	14
13	Chapter 13: Uniting Passions	15
14	Chapter 14: The Impact of Legacy	17
15	Chapter 15: Embracing Change	18
16	Chapter 16: The Joy of Simplicity	19
17	Chapter 17: A Life Well-Lived	20

1

Chapter 1: Beginnings in the City

In the heart of a bustling metropolis, Lila sat in her tiny apartment, the hum of the city acting as the backdrop to her thoughts. She had always been a dreamer, but with the weight of student loans and the pressure to find a stable job, dreams seemed distant. Her heart was torn between pursuing her passion for art and accepting a lucrative corporate offer. As she stared at the blank canvas before her, she wondered if there was a way to marry both worlds.

Her best friend, Sam, a tech enthusiast, often spoke about the possibilities of integrating technology with creativity. "You can code your way through art, Lila. Imagine the endless possibilities," he would say, his eyes lighting up with excitement. Despite his encouragement, Lila felt the familiar pull of doubt. The corporate world promised security, while the artist's life was fraught with uncertainty.

One evening, as the city lights began to twinkle, Lila received a message from an old college professor. "There's an opening for an art director at a tech startup. They're looking for someone with your unique skill set," the message read. Her heart raced. Was this the sign she had been waiting for? The decision weighed heavy on her, but deep down, she felt a spark of hope.

The following morning, with the sunrise casting a golden hue over the city, Lila made her decision. She would go for the interview. As she prepared, she felt a surge of determination. This was her chance to bridge the gap between her passion and the practical world. She stepped out of her apartment, ready to embrace the unknown.

2

Chapter 2: The Tech Startup

Lila's first day at the tech startup was a whirlwind. The office was a vibrant space filled with young, enthusiastic minds working on groundbreaking projects. She felt a mix of excitement and nervousness as she was introduced to the team. They welcomed her with open arms, eager to see how her artistic vision could blend with their technological prowess.

Her role as art director was both challenging and exhilarating. She collaborated with programmers, UX designers, and marketing experts, bringing her unique perspective to the table. Late nights at the office became the norm, but she didn't mind. She was creating something meaningful, something that resonated with her core.

In the midst of this professional chaos, Lila found herself drawn to Ethan, a software developer with a passion for classical music. Their interactions were initially brief, but over time, they found solace in each other's company. Ethan's calm demeanor and thoughtful conversations were a stark contrast to the fast-paced environment of the startup. They began to spend more time together, finding moments of peace amidst the chaos.

As their bond deepened, Lila started to reflect on her journey. She realized that her career choice had not only brought her professional fulfillment but also unexpected romantic connections. It was as if her heart had its own algorithm, leading her to the right people and places at the right time.

3

Chapter 3: Navigating Love and Ambitions

Lila and Ethan's relationship blossomed amidst the backdrop of coding marathons and brainstorming sessions. They found a rhythm in their shared passions and contrasting personalities. Ethan's love for classical music and Lila's artistic flair created a harmonious balance in their lives. However, as their relationship grew, so did the challenges.

Ethan was offered a prestigious fellowship abroad, an opportunity that he had dreamt of for years. It was a defining moment in his career, but it also meant being miles away from Lila. They faced the difficult decision of choosing between their individual ambitions and their relationship. Long nights were spent in deep conversations, trying to navigate the complex emotions and practicalities of their situation.

Lila, on the other hand, was presented with a leadership role at the startup. It was a chance to drive her vision further, but it required her full commitment. She felt torn between supporting Ethan's dreams and pursuing her own. The weight of these decisions pressed heavily on their hearts, testing the strength of their bond.

In a moment of clarity, they decided to support each other's aspirations, even if it meant being apart for a while. They believed that true love could withstand distance and time. With tears and heartfelt promises, they bid each

CHAPTER 3: NAVIGATING LOVE AND AMBITIONS

other farewell, determined to make their relationship work despite the odds. It was a leap of faith, guided by the belief that their love was resilient and enduring.

4

Chapter 4: Spiritual Awakening

As Lila settled into her new role, she found solace in her work. Yet, there was a lingering sense of emptiness, a yearning for something deeper. It was during this time that she stumbled upon a meditation group at a local community center. Intrigued, she decided to give it a try, seeking inner peace and clarity.

The meditation sessions became a sanctuary for Lila, offering a much-needed respite from the chaos of her professional life. Through mindfulness practices and spiritual teachings, she began to reconnect with herself. She discovered that spirituality was not about religion but about finding a deeper connection with her inner being and the world around her.

As she delved deeper into her spiritual journey, Lila began to see her career and relationships through a new lens. She realized that true fulfillment came from aligning her actions with her values and passions. This newfound clarity inspired her to introduce mindfulness practices at the startup, fostering a more balanced and creative work environment.

Lila's spiritual growth also had a profound impact on her relationship with Ethan. They found new ways to connect despite the physical distance, sharing their spiritual insights and supporting each other's personal growth. Their bond transcended the material world, rooted in a deep sense of love and understanding.

5

Chapter 5: Challenges and Resilience

Life at the startup was never short of challenges. The company faced financial hurdles, competitive pressures, and the constant demand for innovation. As a leader, Lila had to make tough decisions, often feeling the weight of responsibility on her shoulders. Yet, she approached these challenges with resilience and a steadfast belief in the vision she had for the company.

Her team looked up to her as a source of inspiration and guidance. Together, they navigated the ups and downs, finding creative solutions to problems and celebrating small victories along the way. The sense of camaraderie and shared purpose kept them going, even during the toughest times.

Meanwhile, Ethan was thriving in his fellowship, making significant strides in his research. Despite the physical distance, he remained a constant source of support for Lila. They continued to find ways to nurture their relationship, from late-night video calls to surprise visits. Their love was a testament to the power of resilience and commitment.

Lila's spiritual practices also played a crucial role in helping her stay grounded and centered. Meditation and mindfulness became daily rituals, providing her with the strength and clarity to face challenges head-on. She realized that true leadership came from within, from a place of authenticity and inner peace.

6

Chapter 6: Finding Balance

As the years passed, Lila and Ethan found a sense of balance in their lives. They had grown both individually and as a couple, navigating the complexities of their careers and relationship with grace and resilience. They had learned to prioritize what truly mattered, finding harmony between their personal and professional lives.

Lila's startup had become a thriving success, known for its innovative approach and positive work culture. She took pride in the impact they were making, both in the tech industry and in the lives of their employees. The company had become a reflection of her values, a place where creativity and mindfulness coexisted.

Ethan had completed his fellowship and returned home with a wealth of knowledge and experiences. He had found a position that allowed him to continue his research while also contributing to the community. Their shared journey had strengthened their bond, and they looked forward to building a future together.

In their personal lives, they continued to explore their spiritual paths, finding joy and fulfillment in the simple moments. They realized that life was not about the destination but the journey, and they were committed to savoring every step along the way. Their love had evolved into a deep, unbreakable connection, rooted in mutual respect and understanding.

7

Chapter 7: New Beginnings

Lila and Ethan's journey had taught them the value of embracing change and new beginnings. As they stood on the threshold of a new chapter in their lives, they felt a sense of excitement and anticipation. They had learned that life was a continuous journey of growth and discovery, and they were ready to face whatever lay ahead.

Lila's startup was expanding, and she was considering new opportunities and partnerships. She had always dreamed of creating a platform that would empower artists and technologists to collaborate and innovate. With the support of her team, she began to explore ways to turn this vision into reality.

Ethan, too, was embarking on a new project that combined his love for music and technology. He was developing a software that would help musicians compose and produce music in innovative ways. It was a perfect blend of his passions, and he was eager to see where it would lead.

Their personal lives were also filled with new beginnings. They had moved into a cozy apartment in a quiet neighborhood, a place they could call their own. They spent weekends exploring the local community, enjoying the simple pleasures of life. It was a time of renewal and growth, and they cherished every moment.

8

Chapter 8: The Power of Connection

One of the most profound lessons Lila and Ethan had learned was the power of connection. Whether it was their connection with each other, with their work, or with their inner selves, these connections brought meaning and fulfillment to their lives.

Lila's startup had become a hub for creative collaboration, attracting artists, technologists, and innovators from all walks of life. The platform she had envisioned was taking shape, and it was transforming the way people approached art and technology. She felt a deep sense of purpose in her work, knowing that their efforts were making a difference. It was a reminder of the power of human connection and collaboration.

Ethan's software project was also gaining momentum. Musicians from around the world were using his tools to compose and produce music in innovative ways. He felt a profound sense of fulfillment in knowing that his work was helping others express their creativity. It was a testament to the impact that passion and dedication could have.

In their personal lives, Lila and Ethan continued to nurture their connection with each other. They found joy in the small moments, from cooking together to taking long walks in the park. Their love had grown deeper, grounded in a strong foundation of trust and understanding. They knew that no matter what challenges came their way, they would face them together.

9

Chapter 9: Overcoming Adversity

Life is never without its challenges, and Lila and Ethan faced their fair share of adversity. The tech industry was constantly evolving, and the startup had to adapt to stay relevant. There were times when financial pressures and competitive threats seemed insurmountable. Yet, Lila's leadership and the team's unwavering commitment helped them navigate these turbulent waters.

Ethan, too, faced obstacles in his journey. There were setbacks in his research, moments of doubt, and the pressure to continuously innovate. But he drew strength from his passion and the support of his loved ones. He learned that failure was not the end but a stepping stone to success.

Together, Lila and Ethan found ways to support each other during these tough times. They leaned on their spiritual practices, finding solace in meditation and mindfulness. They also sought the advice of mentors and peers, realizing that they didn't have to face challenges alone. Their resilience and determination saw them through the darkest moments, emerging stronger and more united.

10

Chapter 10: Celebrating Success

After years of hard work and dedication, Lila and Ethan began to see the fruits of their labor. The startup had become a leader in the industry, known for its innovative solutions and positive impact on the community. Lila took immense pride in what they had achieved, knowing that it was the result of collective effort and vision.

Ethan's software project had also gained widespread recognition. Musicians and artists praised the tools he had developed, and his work was featured in prominent publications. He felt a deep sense of fulfillment in knowing that his efforts were making a difference in the world of music.

They celebrated these successes with their friends and family, reflecting on the journey they had undertaken. It was a time of joy and gratitude, a reminder of the power of perseverance and passion. They knew that their journey was far from over, but they were excited for the future and the possibilities it held.

11

Chapter 11: Giving Back

With their successes, Lila and Ethan felt a strong desire to give back to the community that had supported them. They began to mentor young artists and technologists, sharing their experiences and knowledge. They believed in the importance of nurturing the next generation and fostering a culture of creativity and innovation.

Lila established a scholarship fund for aspiring artists, providing them with the resources and opportunities to pursue their passions. She also organized workshops and events that brought together artists and technologists, encouraging collaboration and cross-disciplinary thinking.

Ethan, too, found ways to give back. He volunteered at local music schools, teaching young students and helping them explore the world of music technology. He also collaborated with nonprofit organizations, using his skills to develop tools that could benefit underprivileged communities.

Their efforts to give back were driven by a deep sense of gratitude and purpose. They wanted to make a positive impact and create opportunities for others to succeed. It was a reflection of their belief in the power of human connection and the importance of supporting one another.

12

Chapter 12: A New Horizon

As Lila and Ethan stood on the brink of a new horizon, they felt a sense of excitement and anticipation. They had come a long way, growing both individually and together. Their journey had been filled with challenges, growth, and profound connections. They knew that the future held endless possibilities, and they were ready to embrace it.

Lila continued to lead the startup with passion and vision, exploring new avenues for innovation. She remained committed to her values, fostering a culture of creativity and mindfulness. Ethan, too, continued to push the boundaries of music technology, finding new ways to inspire and empower musicians.

In their personal lives, they found joy in the simple moments, from morning coffee to watching the sunset. They had built a life that was rich in love, purpose, and fulfillment. Their bond had grown stronger, rooted in a deep sense of trust and understanding.

As they looked ahead, they knew that their journey was far from over. They were excited for the new adventures and opportunities that awaited them. With hearts full of hope and determination, they were ready to face whatever lay ahead, guided by the belief that love, passion, and resilience could overcome any obstacle.

13

Chapter 13: Uniting Passions

As Lila's startup grew, she realized the importance of integrating diverse talents and perspectives. Inspired by her own journey, she sought to create a collaborative environment where artists, technologists, and creatives from different fields could come together. She launched a series of initiatives aimed at fostering cross-disciplinary innovation and creativity.

One of these initiatives was an annual hackathon, bringing together individuals from various backgrounds to solve real-world problems through technology and art. The event became a huge success, drawing participants from around the world. It was a testament to the power of collaboration and the endless possibilities that arose when different passions united.

Ethan played a pivotal role in these initiatives, mentoring young musicians and technologists. He found immense joy in helping others discover their creative potential. Together, they built a community that thrived on mutual support and shared vision. It was a celebration of their journey and the impact they had made.

Their efforts attracted attention from industry leaders and investors, further solidifying their position as innovators in their respective fields. Lila and Ethan remained humble, always focusing on the values that had guided them from the beginning. They knew that their success was not just about individual achievements but about the collective growth of the community they had nurtured.

14

Chapter 14: The Impact of Legacy

As the years went by, Lila and Ethan began to reflect on the legacy they wanted to leave behind. They had achieved remarkable success, but they knew that true impact went beyond personal accomplishments. They wanted to create a lasting change that would benefit future generations.

Lila began to focus on creating sustainable solutions and fostering ethical practices within the tech industry. She collaborated with environmental organizations and social enterprises, using technology to address pressing global issues. Her vision was to create a world where innovation and sustainability coexisted harmoniously.

Ethan, too, was driven by a sense of purpose. He worked on projects that brought music and technology to underserved communities, providing access to creative tools and opportunities. He believed in the transformative power of music and wanted to ensure that everyone had the chance to experience its magic.

Together, they established a foundation that supported initiatives aligned with their values. They funded scholarships, mentorship programs, and community projects, creating a ripple effect of positive change. Their legacy was not just about what they had achieved but about the lives they had touched and the opportunities they had created.

15

Chapter 15: Embracing Change

Change is a constant in life, and Lila and Ethan were no strangers to it. They had learned to embrace change and see it as an opportunity for growth and discovery. As they entered a new phase of their lives, they were faced with decisions that would shape their future.

Lila decided to step down from her leadership role at the startup, passing the baton to a new generation of leaders. It was a difficult decision, but she felt it was time to explore new horizons. She wanted to focus on her artistic pursuits and personal growth, reconnecting with the passion that had ignited her journey.

Ethan, too, was ready for a change. He wanted to delve deeper into his research and explore new avenues for innovation. They both knew that change was not the end but a new beginning, a chance to redefine their paths and discover new passions.

Their love and partnership remained a constant anchor, guiding them through the transitions. They supported each other, knowing that true fulfillment came from following their hearts and embracing the unknown. It was a reminder that life was a journey of continuous evolution, and they were ready to face it together.

16

Chapter 16: The Joy of Simplicity

In their quest for success and impact, Lila and Ethan had also discovered the joy of simplicity. They realized that true happiness was found in the small, everyday moments that brought meaning to their lives. They began to prioritize mindfulness and presence, savoring the beauty of the present.

They spent more time in nature, finding solace in the tranquility of the outdoors. They took up hobbies that brought them joy, from gardening to cooking to painting. These simple pleasures became a source of fulfillment, grounding them in the present and reminding them of the importance of balance.

Their spiritual practices continued to play a vital role in their lives. Meditation and mindfulness became daily rituals, providing a sense of inner peace and clarity. They found joy in connecting with their inner selves and with each other, cherishing the moments of stillness and reflection.

Their home became a sanctuary, filled with love, laughter, and creativity. It was a place where they could be themselves, free from the pressures of the outside world. They knew that true wealth was not measured by material possessions but by the richness of their experiences and the depth of their connections.

17

Chapter 17: A Life Well-Lived

As Lila and Ethan looked back on their journey, they felt a profound sense of gratitude and fulfillment. They had navigated the complexities of career choices, romantic bonds, and spiritual growth with grace and resilience. Their lives had been a tapestry of experiences, woven together by love, passion, and purpose.

They had learned that true success was not about reaching a destination but about embracing the journey. It was about following their hearts, staying true to their values, and making a positive impact along the way. They had created a life that was rich in meaning, filled with moments of joy, growth, and connection.

Their love had grown deeper with each passing year, rooted in a foundation of trust and understanding. They had supported each other's dreams and aspirations, finding strength in their partnership. Their bond was a testament to the power of love and the beauty of shared experiences.

As they stood on the threshold of a new chapter, they knew that their journey was far from over. They were excited for the future and the endless possibilities it held. With hearts full of hope and determination, they were ready to face whatever lay ahead, guided by the belief that love, passion, and resilience could overcome any obstacle.

The Heart's Algorithm: A Story of Career Choices, Romantic Bonds,

and Spiritual Growth

In the bustling heart of a metropolis, Lila is torn between her passion for art and the security of a corporate job. Her journey takes an unexpected turn when she lands a role as an art director at a tech startup, where creativity meets innovation. Alongside her, Ethan, a software developer with a love for classical music, becomes both a professional partner and romantic interest.

Together, they navigate the challenges of career ambitions and romantic connections, making difficult decisions that test the strength of their bond. As they grow individually and together, they embark on a spiritual journey, finding solace in meditation and mindfulness.

Their story is one of resilience, embracing change, and finding joy in simplicity. Through professional successes and personal growth, they learn the importance of connection and the power of love. Lila and Ethan's journey is a testament to the transformative power of following one's passions and staying true to one's values.

Join Lila and Ethan in "The Heart's Algorithm" as they explore the intersections of career, love, and spirituality, and discover that true fulfillment lies in the journey, not the destination.

www.ingramcontent.com/pod-product-compliance
Lightning Source LLC
LaVergne TN
LVHW020509080526
838202LV00057B/6251